JESUS INVITES ME
to
Mass

Text by
Sabine du Mesnil

Illustrations by
Gemma Román

MAGNIFICAT · Ignatius

It's Sunday! Today, Jesus invites you to Mass to celebrate the Lord's Supper! He welcomes you to his house, the church.

As Mass begins, everyone sings! The priest goes to the altar and makes the sign of the cross.

You too make the sign of the cross on your body:

In the name...

...of the Father
who is in heaven,

and of the Son
who came down
to earth,

and of the Holy Spirit
who enfolds us
in his love.

God offers you his peace. Sometimes we need to tell God that we are sorry.

Arguing, pouting, not sharing—these make us feel very sad. But God loves you. He wants to give you his forgiveness and his help.

Lord, have mercy.
Christ, have mercy.
Lord, have mercy.

On Christmas night, angels praised God for the birth of Jesus.

With the words of the angels, you too can glorify God, who is so great and so good that he sent us a Savior!

Glory to God in the highest,
and on earth peace to people of good will.

Now it's time for readings from the Bible.
Sit quietly and listen.
This is the story of God's love
for humankind. God, who is in heaven,
wants to be close to us.
He gives us his Word. God's Word is like
a rainbow stretching between him and us.

The reader says,
The Word of the Lord.
We say,
Thanks be to God.

We all stand up for the Gospel!
Alleluia!
Listen to the life of Jesus!

Make a little cross on our forehead, so that the Gospel will help you to know Jesus,

then on your mouth, that your lips may speak of the living Jesus to those around you,

and then on your heart, to keep his word there like a treasure.

The priest or deacon says,
The Gospel of the Lord.

We say,
Praise to you, Lord Jesus Christ.

All together, we recite the Creed to reaffirm our faith.

I believe in one God, the Father almighty,
maker of heaven and earth.

God created everything! He is your Father, and you are
his child. He is all-powerful because he is Love.

I believe in one Lord Jesus Christ.

God the Son became man to dwell among us.

I believe in the Holy Spirit, the Lord, the giver of life.

God the Holy Spirit helps us to do good.

I believe in one, holy, catholic and apostolic Church.

In the four corners of the world, in every country
and in every language, children say the same Creed.
All the baptized are part of the one Body of Christ,
the Church.

During the Offertory, put some money in the basket as an offering to God. It will help the priest to fill the church with flowers, to care for the poor, and to do many other things. Thank you!

As the priest raises the host and then the chalice, raise up your heart and offer it to the Lord.
Give him your troubles, your joys, your family, and your friends!

The priest says,
Lift up your hearts.

We say,
We lift them up to the Lord.

Jesus offered his life on the cross for our salvation.

At Mass, he once again humbles himself to offer himself for us. The bread becomes the Body of Jesus. The wine becomes the Blood of Jesus. This is the most important moment of the Mass!

The priest repeats the words of Jesus over the bread and the wine:

TAKE THIS, ALL OF YOU, AND EAT OF IT,
FOR THIS IS MY BODY. . . .

TAKE THIS, ALL OF YOU, AND DRINK FROM IT,
FOR THIS IS THE CHALICE OF MY BLOOD. . . .

Can you hear a little bell ringing?
It is Jesus ringing at the door
of your heart.

With one voice, we all say together the prayer of the children of God. Jesus himself taught it to us!

Our Father, who art in heaven,
hallowed be thy name;
thy kingdom come,
thy will be done
on earth as it is in heaven.
Give us this day our daily bread,
and forgive us our trespasses,
as we forgive those who trespass against us;
and lead us not into temptation,
but deliver us from evil.

Before Communion, you can exchange a sign of peace with those sitting next to you. This is God's peace! He wishes for everyone to be gathered together in peace, just like the thousands of grains of flour that make one single loaf of bread.

Lamb of God, you take away the sins of the world, have mercy on us.

Lamb of God, you take away the sins of the world, have mercy on us.

Lamb of God, you take away the sins of the world, grant us peace.

As people are given Communion, they open their hearts like a haven of love to receive Jesus. You can go to the altar as well. If the priest blesses you, it is Jesus saying to you, "I love you, have no fear, I am with you."

Once back in your seat, remain silent. In the quiet of your heart, you can say to Jesus, "I know you are here with us, Jesus, and I love you too!"

Mass is almost over.

As the priest blesses everyone, make a sign of the cross, as you did at the start of the Mass.

The priest says,
Go in peace.

We say,
Thanks be to God.

Jesus is happy when you go to Mass. And he is happy when you speak to him at other times, too, just as you would to your best friend!

In your house, there is a place to sleep and a place to eat. Do you have a place to speak with Jesus? Is there a place with an image of him that you like? There, alone or with your whole family, you can thank Jesus for your day and ask for his help and protection.